Terribly Terrific Tales from around the Table

Lindsay Waugh

Presentation by *BookLeaf Publishing*

Web: www.bookleafpub.com

E-mail: info@bookleafpub.com

ISBN: 9789357614610

First edition 2022

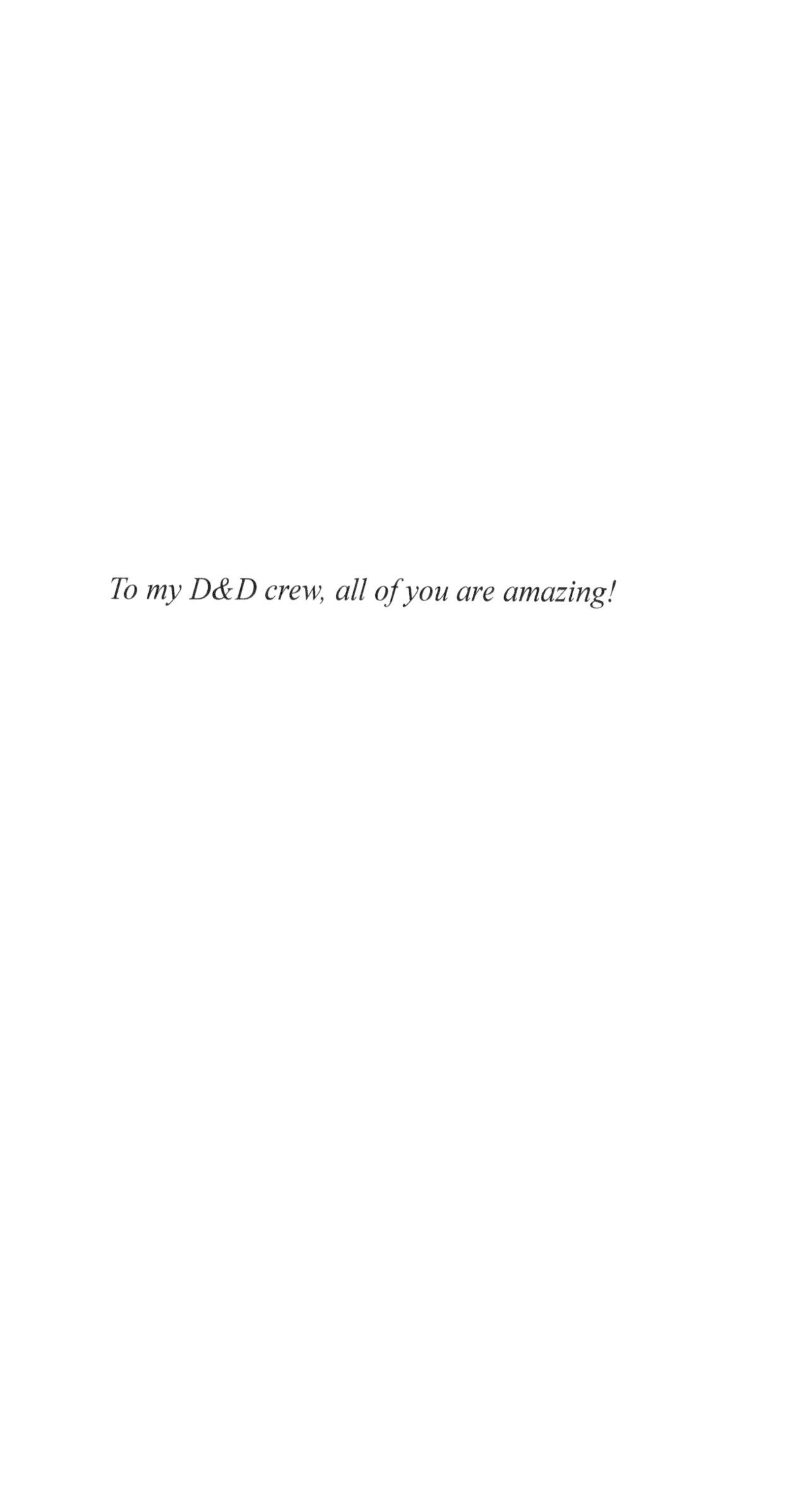

To my D&D crew, all of you are amazing!

ACKNOWLEDGEMENT

First, I would like to thank my three best friends, Paige Miller, who introduced me to this challenge, Kandese Green, who has encouraged me and played in the first game I ran as a Dungeon Master, and Trista Fischer, the "Larry" to my "Bob," and who has been there for me for the past twenty-plus years. Second, I would like to thank Matt Bromley, who didn't hesitate to give me advice and words of wisdom for my first game, and, Matt Kaiser, who has been like a big brother to me in my TTRPG journey, mentoring and encouraging me through my first foray as a DM. And, lastly, and definitely most important, all the gratitude to my husband, Zach, who has tolerated my dice goblin tendencies and supported me, and, my son, Harvey, whose big imagination inspired an entire Discord section of future D&D ideas.

PREFACE

I've been playing tabletop role playing games for several years now, including Dungeons and Dragons, Pathfinder, and Vampire: The Masquerade. Naturally, inspiration flowed when remembering my various adventures with friends from around the table-the camaraderie, the strategy, the tales we still relive. If it weren't for games like D&D, I might not have forged many of the friendships I maintain to this day. To some, it may just be a game. To me, it's been the adventure of a lifetime.

Adventure Calls

Click clack go the dice,
The Adventure calls to me,
Chance and choice await.

Dice Goblin

Multiple sizes and the same old shapes,
Cradled in their holding places,
Small objects seemingly harmless,
Natural ones ensure disgraces.

Start with one set then another,
Obsession I can't ignore,
Shiny math rocks go click clack,
Goblin brain needs all the more!

The weight in my hand satisfies,
As I release them on the table,
Seconds feel like hours passing,
Determining my fate in fable.

Metal, acrylic, stone, and glass,
Like a dragon's collected hoard,
I'm starting to think I have a problem,
But, then again, I'm never bored!

Merchants stock them in their stores,
It's really just a little vice,
Others offer me the strangest looks,
When they see my piles of dice.

Admire my shiny faceted trinkets,
Colors, patterns, and finishes fair,
Yet, when I see a friend in need,
Even this goblin likes to share.

Numbers engraved into the surface,
Decide how a hero will proceed,
If one die betrays its owner,
Then, the next set will take the lead.

Surely I've amassed enough, I think,
My dice needs are all met,
Still another sparks my interest,
It's only one more set.

The Hunt

Breath reveals itself,
Weapons at the ready,
Icy air caresses my cheeks,
Time to move.

Shallow depressions in white,
Wending further between the trunks,
Step light, step quick,
Quarry two steps ahead.

Heart pounding in my ears,
Inhales and exhales hastening,
Silence has descended,
Boots sinking in snow.

Flickers of movement,
A pair of glowing eyes,
Eyes narrow as arrow nocks,
Bowstring anchored against corner.

Growls echo over forest floor,
Fearsome mother defending,
Release the tension,
Bow drops with my breath.

Lithe form pauses an instant,
Smaller shapes follow behind,
A silent thank you,
Vanishing into the early morning.

Sighing as arrow returns to its quiver,
Light starting to crest,
Going home empty-handed,
Somehow, I don't mind.

Are You Familiar with Familiars?

Are you familiar with familiars?
I've stocked so many kinds!
Birds and dogs and cats and beings,
Behold my fabulous finds!

Don't think you want a pet, you say?
How dare, you sir, that's wrong!
Familiars are not pets, I say!
They're more helpful to have along!

Have I finally got your interest?
I have so many on display!
From talkers to magical to the unseen,
I even have some Fey!

No, I didn't glue feathers to that!
Yes, that's its natural hue!
Are you calling me a fraud, good sir?
Well, then, be away with you!

Anyone looking for a familiar?
I'll find your matching pair!
Don't listen to that charlatan!
My wares are real and prices fair!

Bard's Lament

I once asked a pretty young thing,
If she'd give romance a fling,
She said, "Not with you!"
And that was my cue,
A bard's job is only to sing.

In the Shadows

In the shadows she waits,
Breath bated with thrill,
Her quarry strides by,
As she remains still.

A jingle at his side,
Promises great reward,
She slinks up right behind him,
Her presence largely ignored.

Paranoia is kicking in,
He starts to slow his stride,
Gulping, he begins to whistle,
To keep from being terrified.

He whips around,
Eyes wider than a saucer,
Nothing but black,
Stares back at this tosser.

He doesn't realize,
His belt's gotten lighter,
Until he gets home,
In a room that is brighter.

She tests the weight,
Of the gold pouch in hand,
Changing her heading,
Things gone according to plan.

With a smirk on her face,
She pockets the wealth,
No one is the wiser,
Thanks to her stealth.

Oh Rage!

I'm ridiculously strong,
I don't even wear armor,
All the ladies say,
I'm one Hell of a charmer.

In the middle of combat,
I'm a force on my own,
The foes I have defeated,
All lie broken and prone.

Let me tell you a secret,
I harness my rage,
It's like letting an animal,
Out of its cage.

When it's time to let loose,
I start seeing all red,
When I return to my senses,
My adversaries are dead.

If any victory,
Seems too hard to gauge,
Just utter the words,
"I'd like to rage!"

They Met in a Tavern...

They met in a tavern,
One fine autumn day,
In a tavern they met,
To head off to slay.

They met in a tavern,
After a glorious journey,
They had drinks at the bar,
Before watching a tourney.

They met in a tavern,
To celebrate life,
Sat around at a table,
To lament all their strife.

They met in a tavern,
For a tankard of ale,
Raising their beverages,
For a rousing bard's tale.

They meet in a tavern,
It's such a cliche,
But, to meet in a tavern,
Is the adventurer's way.

In the Blue

Journeys in our minds,
Exhilarating our veins,
We live in the blue.

Watch Where You Point That Thing!

Swords and spears and daggers,
Are not a child's play things,
This gouge here in my backside,
Is proof of what I'm saying.

You need to pay attention,
To the weapon at your side,
Don't brandish it so carelessly,
Someone could have died!

This is the fourth or fifth time,
That you've stabbed the ranger,
If you keep on doing this,
You are going to be in danger.

Confiscate his weapon,
Sometimes lessons have to sting,
Everyone get to safety,
WATCH WHERE YOU POINT THAT THING!

Zombies and Wraiths and Liches, Oh My!

Necromancers raise up their friends,
It's not as nice as it sounds,
For now they are among the undead,
Soon they'll be making their rounds!

Zombies shamble along at a pace,
That doesn't seem all that insane,
But, if they manage to catch you,
You might just be losing your brain!

Death wizards summon a specter,
A ghost that's beyond all compare,
Magic will hardly touch one of these,
As it appears from thin air.

Radiant damage will clobber it well,
By a cleric's or paladin's faith,
Just don't let it touch or be near you,
Nothing drains life like a wraith.

When they turn magic upon themselves,
They make a horrible switch,
They've learned how to extend their existence,
They're now a formidable lich.

If I had one piece of friendly advice,
Just pass necromancy on by,
Because if you don't, undead will abound,
Zombies and Wraiths and Liches, Oh My!

The Keening Blade

Edge so sharp, it sings in air,
While seeking the neck beneath your hair,
Wielded by monster foul and fair,
The Keening Blade will soon be there.

If you hear the wailing cry,
Deep, sorrowful, and so high,
Abscond as fast as fleet feet fly,
For if you don't, you'll surely die.

Head detaches, but does not perish,
Fey the Keening Blade does cherish,
Its soul purpose entirely nightmarish,
Mourning blood, a red so garish.

Hiding in shadow, before the sun,
Dullahan brandishes blade for fun,
Sacrifice for the Crooked One,
If you're out in sight, you better run.

As the light begins to fade,
The night is colored an evil shade,
The debt to Crom Cruach is paid,
Beware the cry of the Keening Blade.

Luck of the Dice

17

Natural twenty,
The Dice Gods blessed me with luck,
Dealing Critical.

Voices in my Head

Voices echo in my mind,
Piquing my curiosity,
I can't quite catch the words,
Still, they beckon me to follow.

An accent here, a timbre there,
Figures begin to take shape,
A jaunty half-elf or zany goblin,
I'm taking pencil to paper.

All the pitches high and low,
They tend to talk over one another,
Until the one I'm searching for,
Singles itself out among the din.

I must sound crazy,
I start to wonder myself,
But, these voices serve a purpose,
They breathe life into my characters.

Mimics are Everywhere

An old adventurer shared a joke,
Everyone thought it was droll,
I laughed along with another bloke,
The booze was taking its toll.

The barkeep's cheeks were turning red,
Giggles came from a table,
We travelers all froze with ultimate dread,
The atmosphere turning unstable.

A snicker escaped from a nearby chair,
In the little time we could afford,
"These damn mimics are everywhere,"
Muttered the old hero brandishing his sword.

We followed suit in the blink of an eye,
As the furniture snarled and snatched,
We all stabbed and slashed and cut,
Those mimics were quickly dispatched!

Choose your Character

I once had to ask myself,
Should I play an orc or an elf,
Fighting those dragons,
Earns us our flagons,
Best check that book on the shelf.

Woe is the Unprepared Dungeon Master

Pages upon pages,
Of material to write,
"Perhaps I'll do this later,"
Is this Dungeon Master's plight.

Just a few more days to go,
No ideas come to mind,
I'll find puzzles, traps, and more,
When I'm ready to design.

Night before a session,
I've already gone to bed,
I think I forgot a vital thing,
But nothing's springing in my head.

Morning arrives anew,
I'm in a panic at the thought,
I pack my game materials,
Grasping for anything I've wrought.

Encounters start a little rough,
"Didn't we fight these already?"
"What's the name of this merchant?"
I think his name is Freddy?

And then a sweep of brilliance,
My improv skills kick in,
At the end of a crazy session,
The players are leaving with a grin!

Storming the Keep

Adrenaline pumping,
Our wild hearts thumping,
We wait for the signaling call.

Guards make their rounds,
We avoid making sounds,
It's imperative this stronghold fall.

Warriors crowding,
Someone is shouting,
We press ourselves up to the wall.

A warning bell rings,
Arrows on deadly wings,
Our progress has started to stall.

We finally break through,
Soldiers flood into view,
Hell breaks loose in the hall.

A call for a rally,
With no time to dally,
It's time to rein in this brawl.

With the enemy surrender,
We capture the pretender,
Victory and cheers for us all!

Death of a Comrade

All falls silent around me,
Despite the ringing in my ears,
Relief blooms in my chest,
The defeated settling my fears.

I chance a few steps forward,
Forms appearing through rising dust,
Hand reaching out of its own accord,
Finding purchase on one of us.

Another meets us in the center,
Of chaos, carnage, and blood,
A few more allies materialize,
That bloom swells into a flood.

Low words exchanged among us,
Ensuring the condition of each,
Hands upon faces, necks, shoulders,
Checking everything that's within reach.

A vague sense that something is off,
A notable absence is known,
Frantic search ensues among bodies,
One of ours is out there alone.

I nearly knock one partner over,
When she halts and starts to step back,
I can't comprehend what I'm seeing,
Unprepared for the impact.

Questions arise in mounting alarm,
But, the words have died in my throat,
Eyes can't deny who's lying before us,
Yet, our hearts refuse to take note.

His silhouette form a few feet away,
Lies entirely too still for relief,
One by one, we descend at his side,
Weary and afflicted by grief.

Wails bubble up from somewhere,
In moments I realize it's me,
Another is whispering prayers,
Others are making their silent pleas.

Reality fully sets in as we mourn,
Moved to lift him up off the ground,
Those who don't carry our companion,
Gather his effects scattered around.

The battle ended in victory,
But, we peer around at the cost,
Nothing can dull the edge of the razor,
A cutting reminder of all that's been lost.

No more shall we laugh together,
Though we'll recall the best times we had,
In the throes of our collective anguish,
We weep for the death of a comrade.

Ballad of Jinx

Fur shines brightly in the sun,
Green eyes twinkle with glee,
You'll never find another feline,
As dashing as this tabaxi.

Unable to use her musical voice,
Because of a dastardly spell,
Jinx hunted down her nemesis,
And sent him straight to Hell.

When her party traveled by river,
She was chosen to steer the boat,
Barty's Barge endured a lot,
Jinx was just glad it stayed afloat.

She wields a fan just like a demon,
Blood magic imbuing the blades,
No one can top her speed and grace,
Especially during castle raids.

Jinx once took out six enemies,
While climbing the walls of a keep,
And survived another dimension,
Lesser beings would weep.

Another memory comes to mind,
Something vile to recall,
Jinx was hit with a ray of sickness,
Enemy downed by a rogue hairball.

Jinx then played a vital hand,
With her fellow adventuring team,
Dragonborn conquest and succession,
A leader's mission to build a regime.

Massive army facing a nightmare,
Elder God summoned in their midst,
Fast as thought, Jinx surged on forth,
Dropping Dagon into the Abyss.

You never have to fear again,
When this Ghost Slayer is aloft,
Evil figures tremble greatly,
At the tabaxi named Jinx Croft.

Campaign's End

Dungeon Master's final words,
Players now comprehend,
Hours of weaving tales together,
Our adventure has come to an end.

Pencil, paper, our PCs,
Have been to Hell and back,
Together we've crafted magic,
Memorable and action packed.

Now it's time to take a break,
Laying character sheets down,
They have ventured valiantly,
They deserve to retire unbound.

Campaigns rise and fall throughout,
Emotions following as they will,
Rolling dice and deciding fates,
Has now come to a standstill.

It derives itself from fantasy,
Yet, our adventures seemed like more,
We fought and cheered, side-by-side,
Fostering esprit de corps!